Mother's Day
and Other
Family Days

Crabtree Publishing Company

www.crabtreebooks.com

Crabtree Publishing Company
www.crabtreebooks.com

Author: Reagan Miller
Series and project editor: Sue Labella
Editor: Adrianna Morganelli
Proofreader: Crystal Sikkens
Photo research: Crystal Sikkens
Editorial director: Kathy Middleton
Design: Katherine Berti
       Suzena Samuel (Q2AMEDIA)
Production coordinator and
  Prepress technician: Katherine Berti

Photographs:
Katherine Berti: page 16
Digital Stock: page 1 (background)
Dreamstime: pages 13, 20, 25
iStockPhoto: page 4
Library of Congress: pages 6, 7
Photolibrary: Brand X Pictures: page 27
Shutterstock: cover, pages 1, 5, 8, 9, 10, 11,
    12, 14, 15, 17, 18, 19, 21, 22, 23, 24, 26,
    28, 29, 30, 31 (right)
Wikipedia: Tom White: page 31 (left)

Library and Archives Canada Cataloguing in Publication

Miller, Reagan
    Mother's Day and other family days / Reagan Miller.

(Celebrations in my world)
Includes index.
Issued also in an electronic format.
ISBN 978-0-7787-4930-1 (bound).--ISBN 978-0-7787-4937-0 (pbk.)

    1. Mother's Day--Juvenile literature. 2. Father's Day--Juvenile
literature. 3. Families--Juvenile literature. 4. Handicraft--Juvenile
literature. I. Title. II. Series: Celebrations in my world

HQ759.2.M54 2010   j394.2628   C2010-902757-4

Library of Congress Cataloging-in-Publication Data

Miller, Reagan.
  Mother's Day and other family days / Reagan Miller.
     p. cm. -- (Celebrations in my world)
  Includes index.
  ISBN 978-0-7787-4937-0 (pbk. : alk. paper) -- ISBN 978-0-7787-4930-1
(reinforced library binding : alk. paper) -- ISBN 978-1-4271-9447-3
(electronic (pdf))
  1. Mother's Day--Juvenile literature. 2. Father's Day--Juvenile literature.
3. Families--Juvenile literature. 4. Handicraft--Juvenile literature. I. Title.
II. Series.

  HQ759.2.M55 2011
  306.85--dc22
                            2010016407

Crabtree Publishing Company

www.crabtreebooks.com   1-800-387-7650

Printed in China/082010/AP20100512

Published in Canada
Crabtree Publishing
616 Welland Ave.
St. Catharines, ON
L2M 5V6

Published in the United States
Crabtree Publishing
PMB 59051
350 Fifth Avenue, 59th Floor
New York, New York 10118

Published in the United Kingdom
Crabtree Publishing
Maritime House
Basin Road North, Hove
BN41 1WR

Published in Australia
Crabtree Publishing
386 Mt. Alexander Rd.
Ascot Vale (Melbourne)
VIC 3032

Contents

Celebrating Family

Each family is special and **unique**—no two families are alike! Some families include two parents while others have one parent. Some families have stepmothers or stepfathers.

- This family includes one parent, four children, and a dog. How many members are in your family?

4

People who are part of a family love and care for one another.

Some children live with their grandparents or other caring adults. The one thing all families have in common is love. The people who make up our families, love and care for us.

Holidays such as Mother's Day, Father's Day, and Grandparents Day are special days to celebrate the wonderful people in our families.

Mother's Day History

Mother's Day is a holiday to give thanks to mothers for all the wonderful things they do. The idea for a Mother's Day holiday in the U.S. came from two women.

In 1872, Julia Ward Howe (left) created Mother's Peace Day. This day celebrated peace and **motherhood**.

DID YOU KNOW?

The earliest history of Mother's Day dates back to ancient Greece. The people of Greece held a spring festival to honor the goddess Rhea, the mother of all Greek gods.

By 1910, a woman named Anna Jarvis helped Mother's Day become an **official** holiday in the United States. Many say that Anna's mother had always dreamed of a holiday to celebrate mothers. After her mother passed away, Anna wrote letters to ministers and politicians to gain support for the holiday.

In 1914, U.S. President Woodrow Wilson made Mother's Day an official holiday. In the U.S. and Canada, it is celebrated on the second Sunday in May.

● Anna Jarvis is sometimes called the "mother of Mother's Day."

7

Celebrating Mother's Day

Mother's Day is a day to honor mothers, grandmothers, or other women who show you love and support. There are many ways to show this special person how much she means to you. Many families celebrate this holiday by giving mothers a day to relax.

- Carnations can be different colors, such as red, white, or pink.

DID YOU KNOW?

Anna Jarvis gave out carnations at a church service in honor of her mother. Carnations were her mother's favorite flower. Today, the carnation is the official Mother's Day flower.

8

Make your mother a special meal to show you care.

On this day, many families treat mothers to a special breakfast in bed. Families can help prepare meals or do other chores around the house so mothers do not have to work on their special day. Some people also show their appreciation by giving cards and gifts.

A Mother's Day Craft

Often, the most meaningful gifts are the ones you make yourself. The craft on the next page lets your mother keep you close to her heart!

- Homemade gifts make your mother feel special.

DID YOU KNOW?

You can use your imagination to create a gift for your mother. You can write a poem, sing a song, or draw a picture to show your mother how much you love her.

● Your mother can keep this with her wherever she goes.

Materials:

- 20-gauge wire (found in craft or hardware stores)
- colorful beads
- tape
- pliers

Steps:

1. Ask an adult to use pliers to bend the wire into a "V" shape.

2. Cover both ends of the wire with tape so the ends are not sharp.

3. String the beads onto the wire until only a small piece of wire remains at both ends.

4. Ask an adult to help you bend the beaded wire to form a heart shape. Ask an adult to use the pliers to twist together the ends of the wire.

5. You can attach a safety pin or key ring to the beaded charm.

Father's Day History

In 1910, Sonora Smart Dodd from Spokane, Washington, first suggested creating a holiday to celebrate fathers.

- Because of Sonora Smart Dodd, we now have a special day to honor fathers.

DID YOU KNOW?

In 1972, U.S. President Richard Nixon made Father's Day an official U.S. holiday.

● In Canada and the United States, Father's Day is celebrated on the third Sunday in June.

Sonora's mother died when Sonora was a baby. Sonora's father raised her and her brothers and sisters by himself.

Sonora thought her father and other fathers deserved a special day just as mothers did. Sonora shared her idea with the people in her town, but it took more than 60 years for the idea to become a national holiday.

Celebrating Father's Day

People celebrate Father's Day in many different ways. Because Father's Day takes place in the summer, many people enjoy celebrating the holiday outside in the sunshine. Outdoor activities such as picnics and barbecues are popular on Father's Day.

Many families celebrate Father's Day with a picnic.

Some families enjoy bike riding and hiking on this holiday. In some **communities**, fathers and their children come together to play baseball, soccer, or other sports.

You can give your father a red rose on Father's Day.

DID YOU KNOW?

Red and white roses are the official flowers of Father's Day.

Dad, You Rock!

Show your father you care by making a special paperweight!

Materials:
- a flat, smooth rock (about the size of your palm)
- acrylic paints
- paintbrush
- glitter glue sticks

Steps:

1. Wash your rock with warm, soapy water to remove any dirt. Dry it well.
2. Paint the front of your rock with white acrylic paint. Let the paint dry.
3. Paint "DAD ROCKS" in the center of your rock and decorate around it. Let the paint dry.
4. Trace over the words and any other designs using your glitter glue stick.
5. Let your rock dry before wrapping it up as a gift for dad.

Try making and sending a Father's Day e-card.

DID YOU KNOW?

*You can send an **e-card** to your father on Father's Day. Because e-cards are not made of paper, they are environmentally friendly. Visit the Web site below to see different Father's Day e-cards: www.101fathersday.com*

Grandparents Day

Grandparents Day is a holiday to celebrate grandparents. It is also a day to show love and respect to all **senior citizens** in your community. Grandparents Day was created by a woman named Marian McQuade. She first came up with the idea in 1970.

● Grandparents Day is a good time to spend with senior citizens in your community.

DID YOU KNOW?

The Forget-Me-Not is the official flower of National Grandparents Day.

Spending time with senior citizens in hospitals and nursing homes brightens their day.

McQuade wanted a special day to celebrate grandparents. She also wanted to honor senior citizens living in **nursing homes**. McQuade worked hard to get support for her idea. In 1978, President Jimmy Carter made Grandparents Day an official holiday in the United States. It became an official holiday in Canada in 1995. Grandparents Day is celebrated on the Sunday after Labor Day.

A Grand Day!

Grandparents Day is a special time for grandparents and grandchildren to spend time together.

You can spend time with your grandparents doing activities you both enjoy.

DID YOU KNOW?

There is an official Grandparents Day song. You can visit the link below to learn the words to this song: www.nationalgrandparentsday.com/SongClip.html

Children can learn more about their family history. Ask your grandparents to share stories from when they were young. You might discover that they enjoyed some of the same activities you do. You can also look at photographs from when your grandparents were your age. Grandparents Day is a great time to start holiday **traditions**. Find an activity you both enjoy such as playing board games or hiking. Try doing this activity together every Grandparents Day to make the holiday even more special!

● Looking at photographs shows you what life was like when your grandparents were young.

21

A Grandparents Day Craft

Give your grandparents a hug that stays with them! Follow the instructions on the next page to make a special Grandparents Day gift.

World's **GREATEST** Grandmother

In honor of:

_____

National Grandparents Day 2010

- Make certificates to let your grandparents know how much you love them!

DID YOU KNOW?

Make certificates to honor your grandparents. Visit www.kidsturncentral.com/holidays/ grandparentsday.htm for certificates to print and color.

Materials:

- a long strip of paper
- pencil
- scissors
- markers, glitter, etc.
- ribbon
- ruler

- Give your grandparents a special hug.

Steps:

1. Use a pencil to trace your right hand on the right end of the paper strip and your left hand on the left end.

2. Use a ruler to draw two parallel lines to connect the hands. These are your "arms." Keep the lines far enough apart so you can decorate the "arms."

3. Write a special message to your grandparents along the "arms." Example: "I love you THIS much!"

4. Cut out your "hug."

5. Roll up your cutout and tie a ribbon around it.

Family Day History

Family Day is celebrated in the Canadian provinces of Ontario, Saskatchewan, and Alberta. It is on the third Monday in February. Schools and most businesses are closed.

Some families enjoy spending the day inside playing games on Family Day.

DID YOU KNOW?

Other people around the world also celebrate families. In the Australian Capital Territory, people celebrate Family and Community Day. In South Africa, the day after Easter Sunday is Family Day.

Alberta first celebrated this holiday in 1990. Saskatchewan introduced it in 2007 and Ontario in 2008. The holiday gives people a break during the long winter. In the U.S., Family Day is a state holiday in Arizona.

Family Day is a day off so families can spend time together.

Celebrating Family Day

Because Family Day is in the winter, many families choose to celebrate with outdoor activities such as figure skating, skiing, or tobogganing. Other families prefer to stay warm by choosing indoor activities such as watching movies, playing board games, or working together to prepare a special meal. Museums and theaters often have special concerts and performances that families can attend together.

This family enjoys tobogganing together!

Some families celebrate
by helping others.

No matter what activity you choose,
the most important thing is that your
family is spending time together.

DID YOU KNOW?

*Some families celebrate the holiday by
helping others in need. One way to help
others is by collecting warm winter clothing
and food to give to* **shelters.**

A Family Day Craft

Designing a family crest is a great activity that involves everyone in the family. A family crest is a symbol that represents your family.

- You can research your family history on the Internet.

DID YOU KNOW?

Family Day is a day to be thankful for your family. Write a list of things you most appreciate about each family member. This activity would make a wonderful Family Day tradition!

Materials:

- a large piece of paper
- ruler
- pencil
- scissors
- glue
- art supplies, such as pencil crayons, markers, paint and paint brushes, etc.

Steps:

1. Gather your family members together to plan a design for your family crest. Brainstorm ideas and make a list of things that represent your family, such as foods, traditions, activities, celebrations, flags, etc.

2. Draw a shape of a shield or crest on a large piece of paper. Outline the shape using a black marker or black paint.

3. Leave a space at the top to put your family name. Use a ruler and pencil to divide the rest of the shape into four equal sections.

4. Use your list of ideas to draw or glue pictures in each section of the crest.

5. Write your family motto on the crest.

6. Cut out the crest and hang it in your home.

Around the World

Many countries in the world celebrate holidays that are similar to those featured in this book. Not everyone celebrates them in the same way. Read on to learn more about celebrating some holidays around the world! In England, Simnel cake is a popular Mother's Day dessert.

- Simnel cake is a rich almond cake.

Atole

Tamales

Atoles and tamales are popular foods in Mexico.

In France, Mother's Day is on the last Sunday of May. A special cake shaped like a bouquet of flowers is given to mothers.

In Mexico, Mother's Day is May 10. Churches hold special services to honor mothers. After the service, mothers are served a breakfast with atole and tamales.

DID YOU KNOW?

Make every day a holiday for the people you love! Don't wait for Mother's Day, Father's Day, or other holidays to show people they are important to you.

Glossary

community The people living together in the same area

e-card An electronic greeting card

honor To show respect to someone

motherhood The act of being a mother

nursing homes Places where some older people go to live to be cared for by others

official Recognized by government

senior citizen A person who is past middle age

shelters Places that give food and clothing to people in need

tradition A belief or custom handed down from one generation to the next

unique Special and the only one of its kind

Index